Ready, Set,

Marlene Pérez
Illustrated by Barbara Knutson

Rigby

Today is the bike race.
Marla checks her bike.
Her tires have air,
and her bottle has water.
She puts on her helmet.
She is ready to start.

4

All the children are
at the starting line.
The race is going to start.
"Ready! Set! Pedal!"
yells the man.

Marla rides with all the children.
She wants to win the race today.

6

Marla sees a hill
up the path.
She wants to get
up the hill fast.

Marla stands up to pedal.
She pedals fast.

Then Marla sees a dog
on the path!
She slows down and
toots her horn.
Beep! Beep!
Marla yells, "Look out, dog!"

The dog runs next to Marla.
He wants her to win!

He is running with her.
She can see the finish line!

The children pedal
over the finish line.
The race is done,
and Marla comes in third place.
Her mom and dad are
very happy!

15

Marla didn't win the race,
but she's happy.
She made a new friend.